A Lion Grows Up

by Anastasia Suen
illustrated by Michael L. Denman and William J. Huiett

Thanks to our advisers for their expertise, research, and advice:

Randy Rieches, Curator
Zoological Society of San Diego
San Diego Zoo
San Diego, California

Susan Kesselring, M.A., Literacy Educator
Rosemount–Apple Valley–Eagan (Minnesota) School District

Editorial Director: Carol Jones
Managing Editor: Catherine Neitge
Creative Director: Keith Griffin
Editor: Christianne Jones
Story Consultant: Terry Flaherty
Designer: Nathan Gassman
Production Artist: Angela Kilmer
Page Production: Picture Window Books
The illustrations in this book were created with acrylics

Picture Window Books
5115 Excelsior Boulevard, Suite 232
Minneapolis, MN 55416
877-845-8392
www.picturewindowbooks.com

Printed in the United States of America.

Library of Congress Cataloging-in-Publication Data
Suen, Anastasia.
A lion grows up / by Anastasia Suen ; illustrated by Michael Denman and
William J. Huiett.
p. cm. — (Wild animals)
Includes bibliographical references and index.
ISBN 1-4048-0985-6 (hardcover)
1. Lion—Infancy—Juvenile literature. 2. Lion—Development—Juvenile literature.
I. Denman, Michael L., ill. II. Huiett, William J., 1943- ill. III. Title.
QL737.C23S854 2005
599.757'139—dc22
2005004280

Welcome to the world of wild animals! Follow a baby African lion as he grows up in the savanna. Watch the small cub turn into a strong lion that survives on his own.

Hidden in the tall grass of the African savanna, a lion cub is born. He has one brother and two sisters.

At first, the lion cub can't see and doesn't have any teeth. The small cub is helpless. Like other mammals, he drinks milk from his mother.

A female lion is called a lioness.
A baby lion is called a cub.

5

Surprise! A whole new world is discovered when the lion cub opens his eyes.

In one quick move, the lioness lifts her cub by the scruff on his neck. His mother must protect him from predators.

Lionesses change their cubs' hiding places often. The cubs wait there until the lioness returns from her hunt.

Shhh! The lioness hides her small cub in the long grass. His spots and fur help him hide from predators.

Lion cubs can growl, moan, and purr. They learn to roar when they are older.

8

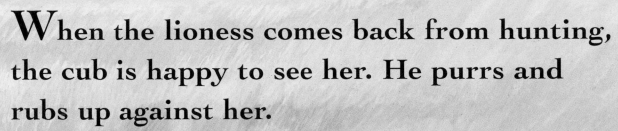

When the lioness comes back from hunting, the cub is happy to see her. He purrs and rubs up against her.

There he goes! The lion cub is now on the move. At six weeks, he has teeth and learns to crawl and walk.

10

Lions learn to run shortly after they learn to walk. A lion can run up to 35 miles (56 kilometers) an hour.

The lioness leads her cubs back to the pride. The lion cub and his sisters and brother meet their father.

Lions love to nap in the warm sun. While the adults are sleeping, the lion cubs play together. They run, jump, and wrestle.

Swat! Tug! The most adventurous cub hits and pulls at his father's tail.

When lions are not hunting, they are usually sleeping.

13

At three months, the lion cub is ready to eat meat. The cub's mother shows him how to hunt for his dinner.

The mother hunts with a team of other lionesses. One lioness scares a zebra, and the others chase it.

Lions hunt at night or early in the morning. Lionesses do most of the hunting for the pride.

At two years old, the cub has turned into a strong lion. He now hunts on his own.

16

The lionesses in the pride help take care of each other's cubs. The lions protect the pride from predators.

17

The lion is all grown up. His mane is full, and the time has come for him to leave the pride. The young lion must find a new pride.

Only lionesses stay in their pride.
Males must move to a new pride.

19

The lion will have to defeat other males in his new pride. Only then can he mate and have a family.

Lions begin to mate when they are about four years old.

After winning the fight, the lion finds a lioness and mates. He becomes a father. A new lion family has started in the African savanna.

① **MANE** The mane helps protect the male's neck during fighting. It also makes him look larger.

② **TAIL** Lions are the only cats with tufts at the ends of their tails.

③ **FUR** Lions have tan fur, which helps them hide among the light-colored savanna grass.

④ **MOUTH** When an adult lion roars, you can hear it up to 5 miles (8 kilometers) away.

⑤ **EYES** A lion's eyesight is five times better than a human's.

Map

There are seven types of lions. The lions in this book are African lions. They live throughout Africa.

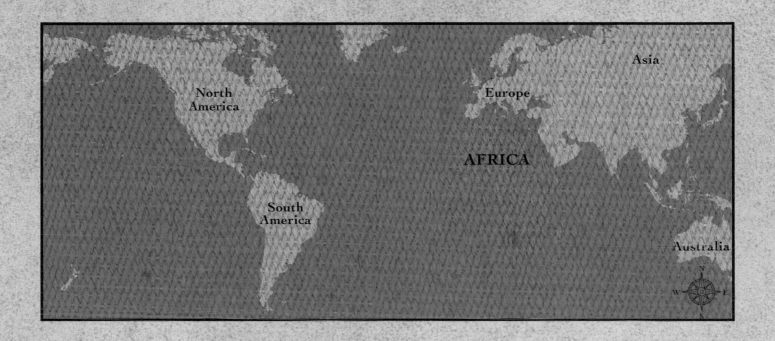

Glossary

cub—a baby lion

lioness—a female lion

mammal—a warm-blooded animal that nurses its young

predator—an animal that hunts and eats other animals

pride—a group or family of lions

savanna—flat, grassy plain that has only a few trees

scruff—the back of the neck

To Learn More

At the Library

Barnes, Julia. *101 Facts About Lions.* Milwaukee: Gareth Stevens Pub., 2004.
Kalman, Bobbie. *The Life Cycle of a Lion.* New York: Crabtree Pub., 2002.
Markle, Sandra. *Lions.* Minneapolis: Lerner Publications, 2004.

On the Web

FactHound offers a safe, fun way to find Web sites related to this book. All of the sites on FactHound have been researched by our staff. *www.facthound.com*

1. Visit the FactHound home page.

2. Enter a search word related to this book, or type in this special code: 1404809856

3. Click on the FETCH IT button.

Your trusty FactHound will fetch the best sites for you!

Index

───── Look for all of the books in the Wild Animals series: ─────

A Baboon Grows Up   A Rhinoceros Grows Up
A Hippopotamus Grows Up   A Tiger Grows Up
A Lion Grows Up   An Elephant Grows Up